THIS JOURNAL
BELONGS TO

# LISA CONGDON

# ONE DRAWING A DAY

## A YEARLONG SKETCHBOOK FOR FINDING YOUR CREATIVE VOICE

CHRONICLE BOOKS
San Francisco

ISBN 978-1-7972-2582-1
Manufactured in China.

10 9 8 7 6 5 4 3

Chronicle books and gifts are available at special quantity discounts to
corporations, professional associations, literacy programs, and other
organizations. For details and discount information, please contact our
corporate/premiums department at corporatesales@chroniclebooks.com
or at 1-800-759-0190.

Chronicle Books LLC
680 Second Street
San Francisco, California 94107
www.chroniclebooks.com

# HOW TO USE THIS BOOK

Usually when people ask me how they can find their artistic voice, I respond simply: Make a lot of art. Truly, your ability to show up, practice, bumble, practice more, then repeat over and over *is* your path. This journal is designed to give you a structure and assignments to practice drawing every day for one year. To help you practice, there is a prompt for each day. Some are literal, and others require a bit more imagination. Some prompts are intentionally repetitive, and others are intentionally weird. Some are about the medium, and some are about the subject. Some are about the way you feel, and others target the way you think. Some are about color, and others are about using space. Practicing in all these different ways will help you to discover what you enjoy and what you find annoying. It will help surface patterns in the way you like to work, including how you use specific marks over and over, and what subject matter you are most comfortable returning to again and again. The goal here is to practice lots of different approaches, subjects, media, colors, and styles, and, as you do, your particular point of view will emerge. Pay attention to where you feel scared or intimidated to try something, then try anyway. Pay attention to feeling in the flow, what makes you happy, and when you feel proud of something. Remember, this is *your* journal. You don't have to show it to anyone! It shouldn't be perfect. In fact, the messier it is, the more it shows you are taking risks, charting new territory, and growing as an artist. Get ready, relax, hold your tools loosely, take your time, and enjoy the process.

## LISA CONGDON

date

**DAY 1** Draw something inspiring you today.

date

**DAY 2** Draw something in a rough style.

date

**DAY 3** Draw your greatest ambition.

date

**DAY 4** Draw your dream art studio.

date

**DAY 5** Draw five things from your bathroom drawer.

date

**DAY 6** Draw your family.

date

**DAY 7** Draw your greatest achievement.

date

**DAY 8** Draw something yellow.

date

**DAY 9**   Draw your values.

date

**DAY 10**   Draw a collection of pencils.

**DAY 11** Draw an experience that changed your life.

**DAY 12** Draw something you desire.

date

**DAY 13** Draw what color looks like.

date

**DAY 14** Draw yourself as a character.

date

**DAY 15** Draw something in your favorite medium.

date

**DAY 16** Draw a greeting card.

**DAY 17** Draw something with a warm palette.

**DAY 18** Draw something with colors you rarely use.

date

**DAY 19** Draw something classic.

date

**DAY 20** Draw yourself at eighty years old.

date

**DAY 21** Draw a snake.

date

**DAY 22** Draw something using paint.

**DAY 23** Draw your future.

**DAY 24** Draw something using hand lettering.

date

**DAY 25** Draw a cloudy sky.

date

**DAY 26** Draw something entirely in your least favorite color.

**DAY 27** Draw something you wish you could draw better.

**DAY 28** Draw something in three colors.

**DAY 29** Draw a zebra.

**DAY 30** Draw something that comforts you.

**DAY 31** Draw an eye five different ways.

date

**DAY 32** Draw a portrait of someone imaginary.

date

**DAY 33** Draw an imaginary collection of things.

date

**DAY 34** Draw your biggest secret.

date

**DAY 35** Draw what you are afraid of.

date

**DAY 36** Draw something you are obsessed with.

date

**DAY 37** Draw what is on your mind today.

date

**DAY 38** Draw something you regret doing.

date

**DAY 39** Draw something organized.

**DAY 40** Draw something you would like everyone to know about you.

**DAY 41** Draw an imaginary character.

**DAY 42** Draw something using three different media.

**DAY 43** Draw a piece of wrapping paper.

date

**DAY 44** Draw something beautiful.

date

**DAY 45** Draw a design for a coffee mug.

date

**DAY 46** Draw sunshine five different ways.

date

**DAY 47** Draw your culture.

date

**DAY 48** Draw something that demonstrates repetition.

date

**DAY 49** Draw something with a cool palette.

date

**DAY 50** Draw courage.

date

**DAY 51** Draw a T-shirt design.

date

**DAY 52** Draw something in nontraditional colors.

date

**DAY 53** Draw something that fills only a quarter of the page.

**DAY 54** Draw something striped.

**DAY 55** Draw your favorite pastime.

**DAY 56** Draw a design for a bandana.

**DAY 57** Draw something with only the color orange.

date

**DAY 58** Draw something in colors you rarely use.

date

**DAY 59** Draw yourself without looking at a mirror or photo.

**DAY 60** Draw something that fascinates you.

**DAY 61** Draw a quilt.

**DAY 62** Draw a mushroom five different ways.

**DAY 63** Draw a new package design for laundry detergent.

**DAY 64** Draw something that shows contrast.

**DAY 65** Draw a hand three different ways.

**DAY 66** Draw how you are feeling today.

**DAY 67**  Draw the ingredients for your favorite meal.

**DAY 68**  Draw your next adventure.

date

**DAY 69** Draw something in a spooky style.

date

**DAY 70** Draw something that you honor.

date

**DAY 71** Draw a landscape.

date

**DAY 72** Draw something with bright colors.

date

**DAY 73**  Draw something weird.

date

**DAY 74**  Draw something with a gradation of color.

date

**DAY 75**  Draw a recent mistake.

date

**DAY 76**  Draw something silly.

**DAY 77** Draw something with just geometric shapes.

**DAY 78** Draw something with only lines.

date

**DAY 79** Draw something you think you cannot draw.

date

**DAY 80** Draw your obsessions.

**DAY 81** Draw something for only five minutes.

**DAY 82** Draw a pattern for something you'd like to make out of fabric.

**DAY 83** Draw a matchbox.

**DAY 84** Draw something abstract.

date

**DAY 85** Draw your favorite toy as a child.

date

**DAY 86** Draw something blue.

**DAY 87** Draw something from your imagination.

**DAY 88** Draw a geometric pattern.

date

**DAY 89** Draw something using numbers.

date

**DAY 90** Draw an animal in clothing.

date

**DAY 91** Draw something repulsive.

date

**DAY 92** Draw tension.

**DAY 93** Draw something with more than two eyes.

date

**DAY 94**  Draw shame.

date

**DAY 95**  Draw a dream.

date

**DAY 96** Draw something you wish you could begin doing now.

date

**DAY 97** Draw something you think about when your mind wanders.

date

**DAY 98** Draw a pile of rocks.

date

**DAY 99** Draw an arrangement of things you find around your house.

date

**DAY 100**   Draw a note to your eighty-year-old self.

date

**DAY 101**   Draw an ear three different ways.

date

**DAY 102** Draw something you are currently making.

date

**DAY 103** Draw an imaginary greeting card that you would like to receive.

date

**DAY 104**   Draw something from your life today.

date

**DAY 105**   Draw yourself with your eyes closed.

date

**DAY 106** Draw something inspired by a folk tradition.

date

**DAY 107** Draw your best friend.

date

**DAY 108**  Draw something you feel you can draw with confidence.

date

**DAY 109**  Draw a design for a tote bag.

**DAY 110** Draw something in a loose style.

**DAY 111** Draw something with only curved shapes.

 date

**DAY 112** Draw an animal.

date

**DAY 113** Draw something wet.

date

**DAY 114**  Draw your childhood.

date

**DAY 115**  Draw something mimicking a fad or trend.

date

**DAY 116**  Draw something that includes mountains.

date

**DAY 117**  Draw something in the style of an artist you love.

date

**DAY 118**   Draw something using a ballpoint pen.

date

**DAY 119**   Draw something precise and controlled.

**DAY 120** Draw a new wrapper for your favorite chocolate.

**DAY 121** Draw something with dimension.

date

**DAY 122** Draw a piece of fruit.

date

**DAY 123** Draw your greatest triumph.

**DAY 124** Draw a song you enjoy.

date

**DAY 125**  Draw as many ideas as you can fit onto the page.

date

**DAY 126**  Draw a floral pattern.

date

**DAY 127** Draw your wildest dream.

date

**DAY 128** Draw something repetitive.

**DAY 129**  Draw yourself looking in the mirror.

**DAY 130**  Draw a leaf three different ways.

**DAY 131** Draw something in a romantic style.

**DAY 132** Draw nature.

date

**DAY 133** Draw a nose three different ways.

date

**DAY 134** Draw waves.

**DAY 135**  Draw something with alternating strokes.

**DAY 136**  Draw something that fills only half the page.

date

**DAY 137** Draw your biggest lie.

date

**DAY 138** Draw your favorite music.

date

**DAY 139** Draw a sheep.

date

**DAY 140** Draw something that conveys rhythm.

date

**DAY 141** Draw something monotonous.

date

**DAY 142** Draw a dog.

▶▶▶▶▶▶▶▶▶▶▶▶▶▶▶▶▶▶▶▶▶▶▶▶▶▶▶▶▶▶▶  _____
date

**DAY 143**  Draw something that you recently learned how to draw.

▶▶▶▶▶▶▶▶▶▶▶▶▶▶▶▶▶▶▶▶▶▶▶▶▶▶▶▶▶  _____
date

**DAY 144**  Draw twenty-five triangles in a pleasing arrangement.

date

**DAY 145**  Draw yourself in twenty years.

date

**DAY 146**  Draw something as hyperrealistic as you can.

**DAY 147** Draw something using a tool that you don't normally use.

**DAY 148** Draw something that is stuck.

date

**DAY 149** Draw something in a warm palette.

date

**DAY 150** Draw something in monochrome.

**DAY 151** Draw something that you wish you were doing right now.

**DAY 152** Draw four hand gestures.

**DAY 153**   Draw something in your least favorite medium.

**DAY 154**   Draw something smaller than a penny.

date

**DAY 156**   Draw something that makes you feel embarrassed.

date

**DAY 157**   Draw something that includes words.

**DAY 158** Draw something on a grid.

**DAY 159** Draw something you wish you had done differently.

**DAY 160**  Draw an apple three different ways.

date

**DAY 161**  Draw a design for a sticker.

**DAY 162** Draw your favorite symbols.

**DAY 163** Draw your goals.

date

**DAY 164**   Draw your favorite beverage.

date

**DAY 165**   Draw a vegetable.

**DAY 166** Draw something modern.

**DAY 167** Draw something you have quit.

date

**DAY 168**   Draw something true about you.

date

**DAY 169**   Draw a symbol for your life.

**DAY 170**  Draw the best gift you have ever received.

**DAY 171**  Draw a pattern with only half circles.

**DAY 172**  Draw yourself doing your dream job.

**DAY 173**  Draw something in a playful style.

**DAY 174** Draw something with three colors or fewer.

**DAY 175** Draw something wavy.

date

**DAY 176**  Draw a portrait of someone you don't know.

date

**DAY 177**  Draw something you wish you had drawn last week.

**DAY 178**  Draw an orange three different ways.

**DAY 179**  Draw something that plays with color value.

date

**DAY 180** Draw a famous painting.

date

**DAY 181** Draw your favorite words.

date

**DAY 182** Draw a sunset.

date

**DAY 183** Draw whatever you want today. Listen to your internal desire.

date

**DAY 184**  Draw a note to your ten-year-old self.

date

**DAY 185**  Draw your reasons for making art.

date

**DAY 186**  Draw something that fills the entire page.

date

**DAY 187** Draw your favorite dinner.

date

**DAY 188** Draw an abstract pattern.

date

**DAY 189** Draw something meaningful.

date

**DAY 190** Draw wood grain.

date

**DAY 191**  Draw something you are currently planning.

date

**DAY 192**  Draw your favorite art supplies.

**DAY 193**   Draw something that represents your style.

**DAY 194**   Draw something you are excited about.

date

**DAY 195**  Draw something that happened to you yesterday.

date

**DAY 196**  Draw something you wish you could draw every day.

**DAY 197** Draw something dull.

**DAY 198** Draw your biggest mistake.

**DAY 199** Draw a uniform.

**DAY 200** Draw something from a photo reference.

**DAY 201** Draw something that bores you.

**DAY 202** Draw five different insects.

date

**DAY 203** Draw something you believe to be true about the world.

date

**DAY 204** Draw something by your favorite artist.

**DAY 205** Draw five kitchen tools.

**DAY 206** Draw self-doubt.

date

**DAY 207** Draw something with only lines.

date

**DAY 208** Draw yourself in red and blue.

date

**DAY 209** Draw something that is hard for you.

date

**DAY 210** Draw a figure.

date

**DAY 211** Draw your home.

date

**DAY 212** Draw curiosity.

date

**DAY 213**  Draw music you enjoy.

date

**DAY 214**  Draw a collection of shells.

date

**DAY 215**  Draw something you think about nearly every day.

date

**DAY 216**  Draw peace.

**DAY 217** Draw twenty-five circles in a pleasing arrangement.

**DAY 218**  Draw something using only the color black.

**DAY 219**  Draw a piece of art inspired by your favorite artistic influence.

date

**DAY 220** Draw something that makes you feel uncomfortable.

date

**DAY 221** Draw something you saw when you were outside in the world this week.

date

**DAY 222** Draw the last thing you purchased.

date

**DAY 223** Draw three things from your refrigerator.

**DAY 224** Draw your fashion.

**DAY 225** Draw something using four different media.

▶▶▶▶▶▶▶▶▶▶▶▶▶▶▶▶▶▶▶▶▶▶▶▶▶▶▶▶▶

date

**DAY 226**  Draw something using a food or liquid from your kitchen.

▶▶▶▶▶▶▶▶▶▶▶▶▶▶▶▶▶▶▶▶▶▶▶▶▶▶▶▶▶

date

**DAY 227**  Draw vulnerability.

**DAY 228**  Draw something old-fashioned.

**DAY 229**  Draw something with woolly texture.

date

**DAY 230** Draw a representation of your culture.

date

**DAY 231** Draw something with a fluffy texture.

**DAY 232**   Draw a collection of scissors.

**DAY 233**   Draw something with only thick lines.

**DAY 234**  Draw something warm.

**DAY 235**  Draw something you want to explore.

date

**DAY 236**  Draw a rose three different ways.

date

**DAY 237**  Draw a daisy three different ways.

date

**DAY 238**  Draw your favorite season.

date

**DAY 239**  Draw a rabbit.

date

**DAY 240**  Draw someone close to you.

date

**DAY 241**  Draw something that is identifiably in your own style.

date

**DAY 242** Draw something from your favorite period in history.

date

**DAY 243** Draw your greatest teacher.

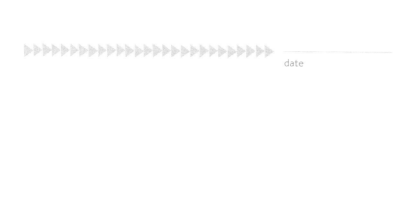

date

**DAY 244** Draw something that requires monotonous repetition.

date

**DAY 245** Draw something you are afraid of.

date

**DAY 246** Draw something in a cool palette.

date

**DAY 247** Draw your favorite food.

**DAY 248** Draw an album cover.

**DAY 249** Draw something loose and messy.

**DAY 250** Draw something you feel indifferent toward.

date

**DAY 251** Draw being vulnerable.

date

**DAY 252** Draw your greatest hope.

date

**DAY 253**  Draw something that conveys movement.

date

**DAY 254**  Draw a book cover.

**DAY 255** Draw something that gives you anxiety.

**DAY 256** Draw a note to someone you want to thank.

**DAY 257** Draw something that shows a vanishing point.

**DAY 258** Draw a bowl of fruit.

date

**DAY 259**  Draw something using two different media.

date

**DAY 260**  Draw something that you think you are bad at drawing.

 date

**DAY 261** Draw your greatest heartbreak.

date

**DAY 262** Draw something with dots.

date

**DAY 263** Draw a memory.

date

**DAY 264** Draw your pass to a dream event.

date

**DAY 265** Draw the last thing you took a photograph of on your phone.

date

**DAY 266** Draw something messy.

**DAY 267**  Draw something in a medium that you have little
experience using.

**DAY 268**  Draw your favorite breakfast.

date

**DAY 269** Draw something in comic-book style.

date

**DAY 270** Draw a sunset.

date

**DAY 271** Draw a self-portrait of yourself as an artist.

date

**DAY 272** Draw something you enjoy doing alone.

date

**DAY 273**   Draw something you wish you could learn to do.

date

**DAY 274**   Draw joy.

▶▶▶▶▶▶▶▶▶▶▶▶▶▶▶▶▶▶▶▶▶▶▶▶▶▶▶▶▶▶▶▶

date

**DAY 275**   Draw something in your favorite color.

▶▶▶▶▶▶▶▶▶▶▶▶▶▶▶▶▶▶▶▶▶▶▶▶▶▶▶▶▶▶▶

date

**DAY 276**   Draw a mouth three different ways.

date

**DAY 277** Draw something with only thin lines.

date

**DAY 278** Draw something sharp.

**DAY 279** Draw a list of things you are interested in learning more about.

date

**DAY 280** Draw two different hand gestures.

date

**DAY 281** Draw a fantasy.

date

**DAY 282** Draw a rainbow.

date

**DAY 283** Draw a doodle.

date

**DAY 284**  Draw your favorite outfit.

date

**DAY 285**  Draw a collection of eyeglasses.

**DAY 286**  Draw your identity.

**DAY 287**  Draw something using a pencil.

 date

**DAY 288**  Draw confidence.

 date

**DAY 289**  Draw a chair three different ways.

**DAY 290** Draw something with only the color green.

**DAY 291** Draw something with only the color pink.

date

**DAY 292**  Draw your favorite lunch.

date

**DAY 293**  Draw your most pressing questions.

**DAY 294**  Draw your favorite book.

**DAY 295**  Draw your favorite smells.

**DAY 296** Draw talent.

**DAY 297** Draw your inner voice.

date

**DAY 298** Draw something in your dream style.

date

**DAY 299** Draw a recipe for something delicious.

 date

**DAY 300** Draw a note to someone you want to apologize to.

date

**DAY 301** Draw something cold.

date

**DAY 302** Draw a letter to your greatest artistic influence.

date

**DAY 303** Draw something that makes you feel vulnerable.

date

**DAY 304** Draw something in the style of an artist whose work you do not like.

date

**DAY 305** Draw a still life.

▶▶▶▶▶▶▶▶▶▶▶▶▶▶▶▶▶▶▶▶▶▶▶▶▶▶▶▶▶▶▶▶▶▶

**DAY 306** Draw something you are proud of.

▶▶▶▶▶▶▶▶▶▶▶▶▶▶▶▶▶▶▶▶▶▶▶▶▶▶▶▶▶▶▶▶▶

**DAY 307** Draw your regrets.

date

**DAY 308**  Draw something that includes more than three layers.

date

**DAY 309**  Draw anxiety.

**DAY 310** Draw your childhood bedroom (if you had more than one, draw the one you remember the most clearly).

date

**DAY 311** Draw the shoes you are wearing today.

date

**DAY 312** Draw something with more than one medium.

date

**DAY 313** Draw your favorite flower.

date

**DAY 314** Draw a cat.

date

**DAY 315**  Draw as many colors as you can fit into this space.

date

**DAY 316**  Draw your hopes.

**DAY 317** Draw something that demonstrates harmony.

**DAY 318** Draw facial features.

date

**DAY 319** Draw your greatest failure.

date

**DAY 320** Draw a passion.

▶▶▶▶▶▶▶▶▶▶▶▶▶▶▶▶▶▶▶▶▶▶▶▶▶▶▶▶▶▶

date

**DAY 321**  Draw something that is saturated.

▶▶▶▶▶▶▶▶▶▶▶▶▶▶▶▶▶▶▶▶▶▶▶▶▶▶▶▶▶

date

**DAY 322**  Draw a portrait of someone you know.

date

**DAY 323** Draw something in a rigid style.

date

**DAY 324** Draw something with only the color beige.

date

**DAY 325** Draw something with at least twelve different colors.

date

**DAY 326** Draw something in two colors.

**DAY 327** Draw an homage to your favorite genre of art.

**DAY 328** Draw a lie.

date

**DAY 329** Draw something from history.

date

**DAY 330** Draw something in four colors.

date

**DAY 331** Draw clouds.

date

**DAY 332** Draw your favorite place.

date

**DAY 333** Draw something shiny.

date

**DAY 334** Draw your favorite animal.

date

**DAY 335**  Draw a map of your life.

date

**DAY 336**  Draw something that includes a body of water.

date

**DAY 337** Draw something magical.

date

**DAY 338** Draw something you used to be afraid of.

date

**DAY 339** Draw perseverance.

date

**DAY 340** Draw something that makes you feel happy.

**DAY 341**  Draw a pattern.

date

**DAY 342** Draw an arrangement of fruit.

date

**DAY 343** Draw something that uses your best drawing skill.

date

**DAY 344** Draw something trendy.

date

**DAY 345** Draw what being "in the flow" looks like for you.

 date

**DAY 346** Draw something that is flowing.

date

**DAY 347** Draw something with repeating imagery.

▶▶▶▶▶▶▶▶▶▶▶▶▶▶▶▶▶▶▶▶▶▶▶▶▶▶▶▶▶▶ _____

date

**DAY 348** Draw something from the grocery store.

▶▶▶▶▶▶▶▶▶▶▶▶▶▶▶▶▶▶▶▶▶▶▶▶▶▶▶▶▶▶ _____

date

**DAY 349** Draw a bird three different ways.

**DAY 350** Draw your artistic influences.

**DAY 351** Draw play.

 date

**DAY 352** Draw something you believe to be true about yourself.

 date

**DAY 353** Draw the most important person in your life.

date

**DAY 354**  Draw kindness.

date

**DAY 355**  Draw a coffee cup three different ways.

date

**DAY 356**  Draw love.

date

**DAY 357**  Draw something with texture.

**DAY 358**  Draw a bear.

**DAY 359**  Draw something that depicts dimension.

date

**DAY 360** Draw something in a flat style.

date

**DAY 361** Draw something outside your window.

date

**DAY 362**  Draw your mood today.

date

**DAY 363**  Draw something red.

**DAY 364**  Draw something serious.

**DAY 365**  Draw something you wish you could begin doing now.

# 10 STEPS TO BUILDING SKILL

1. BEGIN
2. PRACTICE
3. KEEP SHOWING UP
4. PRACTICE MORE
5. STRETCH YOURSELF
6. PRACTICE
7. PRACTICE
8. NOTE YOUR IMPROVEMENT
9. PRACTICE MORE
10. REPEAT